My Journey
A lifetime of verse

My Journey
A lifetime of verse

Copyright © 2007 by Trina L.C. Sonnenberg
Photographs by, Jeff Sonnenberg

All rights reserved worldwide. No part of this book may be used or reproduced in any manner whatsoever, without the express written consent of the author.

Trina L.C. Sonnenberg
www.trinaschiller.ws
P.O. Box 481
Nucla, Colorado USA

ISBN: 978-0-6151-6405-2

This book was begun, more than 20 years ago, as a way of coping with the dips and swells of life. My Journey is a collection of poems, born of tears and laughter.

This book is dedicated to all of those who have stood by me through my growing pains, and have shared this journey with me. Special appreciation to my beloved husband, who has provided me with much inspiration and the happiest years of my life.
I love you all.
~Trii

Author's Note:

Dear Reader,

I used writing as a coping mechanism during my years as a battered woman. This book is the result of that personal struggle and has been published as a way of offering solidarity and hope to others who are in a similar situation.

The poems in this book are not in any particular chronological order. Some of them date back as early as the 1980's, and others are as recent as 2007.

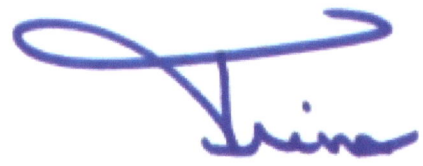

Some Days

Some days are better than others.
Yet even on the darkest days, it is true…
One thing shines through the cloud cover -
Memory of your eyes so blue.

Miles may separate us now and then,
Thoughts of you are ever present, inside my head -
Always anticipating when I will see you again;
Wondering what the future holds; knowing my feelings won't end.

Your passion exhilarates me; you are most intriguing -
The mystery surrounding you is to me, quite tantalizing.
When sadness swallows me,
I am freed by your memory.

You may hate all of this mushy stuff…
But you inspire me to write, so Charlie… Tough Luck!

Some days are better than others…
Thoughts of you break through the cloud cover.

~~~~
Let Me Go

My brain is fried,
My heart is dry,
I've shed all the tears that I had to cry.

Why can't you let me go?
Does it pain you that much, to see me grow?

The ruins you clutched have slipped through your hand.
Now you are left to watch me roam the land.

I loved you once, but feel it no more.
It is time for me to lock the door.

~~~

You don't have to love me…
That you care is enough.
I love you more, each time I look at you.
You are kind, thoughtful and true..
You allow me to love you.
My heart has not known this kind of joy before.
There's nothing about you I do not adore.

You can never know just how precious you are to me…
How thankful I am to share your life.
You don't have to love me.

~~~

In the hills they united
Under blue skies, with the Lord as their witness,
To their hearts' solemn vow;
They give to the other, not just the future…but the here and now.
In faith and love, kneeling upon a flower carpeted clearing;
And an accompaniment of birds -
Their lovely voices… oh the song they sing!

As the sun slips down;
The final blessing said -
To consummate a dream…
They take to their matrimonial bed.

My Secret

I am beautiful, smart, healthy and strong…
I am a universal magnet and this is my song.

Riches come to me effortlessly, every day.
I am a powerhouse; I am on my way.
I have the best of everything,
And give thanks each morning I rise.
Life is a gift, abundance the prize.

I am beautiful, smart, healthy, and strong…
I am a universal magnet and this is my song.

I sing from my soul -
The joy within me cannot be contained.
I am free to fly, my life unrestrained.

I am the master of my life, not fate.
I set the course to be sailed, with love, not hate.

I give love, laughter, and understanding:
Returning to me a hundred fold…
So to you, my friend,
My secret is told.

I am beautiful, smart, healthy, and strong…
I am a universal magnet and this is my song.

~~~~

Gatekeeper

Gatekeeper, Gatekeeper, let me come through.
My time here is done.
I have paid my dues.
My quest for happiness has ended in pain.
My time has been wasted,
My efforts in vain.

Gatekeeper, Gatekeeper, let me pass by.
I haven't the heart to keep living a lie.

Gatekeeper, Gatekeeper, grant my wish with these final words spoken…
I've lost at life; my will has been broken.

~~~~

I am starving for affection,
I hunger for a warm embrace -
Longing gazes, and laughter -
I thirst for a tender kiss.
I search for my bliss.

I crave words of love, appreciation, and kindness.
My life is lacking playfulness.
I am empty and sightless.

This nourishment has been denied me too long.
I know not how to fortify my life -
I know not how to be strong.

My heart grows weary -
The blood in my veins grows cold.
My humor has deserted me.
I feel incredibly old.

Each time I reach for the desires of my heart,
The cup is pulled from my fingers.
Parched pain is all that lingers.

Is there no oasis in this desert for me?
Not even some shade, beneath a tree?

~~~

I am up here staring at my walls four.
Sitting and staring is such a bore.
I am sitting up here with nothing to do…
Wishing, waiting, wanting you.
Wanting you to walk through my door,
For then I would sit and stare no more.
Suddenly I hear steps, one then two…
Oh my Darling, is it you?

Second Chance

No, I have not fallen in love with you for a second time.
Just the sound of your name has always made my heart chime.

I promised to love you forever, and always, so I kept it in a safe place.
I kept my love for you in an unbreakable space.

That love has been set free and mends many broken fragments.
All that time in storage, my love never grew stagnant.

Like sunshine upon my face, my happiness radiates,
I've asked God, many times, why He made me wait.

Like pieces of a puzzle, our lives seem to fit.
My life is so much more, now that you are in it.

~~~

Once again, I sit and wonder about you.
Why do you do and say the things that you do?

Why are your words so taunting and callous?
What did I do to deserve such malice?

You say you love me; your actions say it's a lie.
Each time you chastise, a part of me dies.

Your touch, once gentle, seemed to be nature.
Now awkwardness is your stature.

I feel that if you love me, you must not like me too much.
I long for that long-ago warm touch.

So, I sit here and wonder about you…
Why do you do and say what you do?

~~~

You don't care about my pain,
You walk away from my tears…
You chastise my cries,
You make fun of my fears.

All you know is your own little world -
You won't venture out,
Or let anyone in…
Your eyes see doubt -
Only you can win.

There is never a gentle embrace,
Never a loving touch.
You've moved miles away, and I miss you so much.

You wore a mask when we met -
Your face I did not see…
Oh, but off it came, once you knew you had me.

Off came the mask, and up went the wall…
As more time passes, I barely know you at all.

I won't hurt you, I say…
But my words mean nothing to you.
Is there no way to prove I am true?

~~~

The emptiness doesn't show,
But the loneliness does grow -
Within me.

I've been alone forever, it seems,
But I still had my dreams,
To keep me.

I had arms, if need be,
Humor to cheer me -
Unable to see how to be happy.

With all of the things that marriage is meant to bring,
I was still always alone.
Yet the silence is unbearable,
Only my anguish is audible,
Empty is my home.

~~~

Why did you do this to me?
Why couldn't you leave me be?
I never changed, why did you?
Do you really know what you've put me through?

We could've had it all,
But you had to drop the ball.
We could've had everything and plus…
But you didn't care about us.

All I can do now is ask questions,
I can't even cry…
Not even for a love that died.

Tears of humiliation, those I have shed.
For what you have done to me, I've wished you dead.

Now I rue the day I let you into my life.
I curse the day I became your wife.

Get the help you so desperately need.
Remember…
Broken hearts bleed.

~~~~

My life has now come full turn.
What, in all of this, did I learn?

The life I lead now is not much different than the one I left.
Once more, I have become a woman kept.

I do his bidding; keep house and home.
I am imprisoned, heart-sick, and alone.

The high wire I walk is slack and unstable.
Yet I walk it with care,
As best as I am able.

Should I misstep, I'd plunge into the abyss…
Is mine a life that someone would miss?

What have I learned…?
Things do not change.
Perhaps the players, but the game is still the same.

~~~

Sometimes I look at him when he doesn't see.
There is a boy, in a man's body, before me.

When our eyes meet, he becomes frigid; not just a bit beyond my touch -
Yet when he looks away, he transforms so much.
He returns to the man of long ago -
He, who embraced my heart…
The man I once knew, and loved from the start.

It is my desire for this man to look back at me.
Instead of stealing a glimpse, when he does not see.

~~~~
### *New Day*

My thoughts are but a misty morn -
The sun not yet shining, the new day not born.
I cannot chose which path to follow.
All that is certain is that inside I'm hollow.

I have choices to make.
Am I up to the test?
I'll do what I can and to Hell with the rest.

~~~

A wicked life I must have lead,
Long ago before I died.
I remember not what path I followed,
Only that this life's been tried.
What evil deeds does my past contain?
Troubled by my dreams, my thoughts...
My purpose yet unclear-
Surely I was severe.

I walk through this life clouded, unsure;
Not understanding where to go.
Why, I do not know.
So much have I still to give,
And want to do in turn.
Why then am I lonesome?
What have I yet to learn?
Do I now pay for sins committed in lives past?
From some crooked road, I've trod.
I beg you Lord; I pray answer me.
Deliver me from this nod.

Copyright © C. Andy 2002

~~~
## *Always With You*

**Where the Time Goes…**

When you were one, you'd come visit me -
At work, where I'd most always be.

By the time, you were three,
Our world was just you and me -
Mommy and Jeri…
Alone at sea.

At the age of five, our roller coaster took a dive;
Together, we made it out alive.

However, when you'd turned seven,
God blessed us from Heaven.
Brand new lives were we given.

Eight saw you become a big brother -
By nine, one like no other.

Thirteen is when you really hit the ground running -
Watch out world… Jeri's coming!

These last few years I've seen you truly come into your own.
I am so very proud of how you have grown.

~~~~

You are a part of me…

The years have passed so quickly, I hardly know where they've gone.
From the day you were born, I knew you were a special someone.
I've watched you grow from just a babe, to a wonderful young man;
Of you I am so proud.
With confidence and honor, you stand out from the crowd.
I know your destiny holds many great things-
It is with pride and love, for you, that my heart sings.

It has been many years since you stopped holding my hand, yet I'm not ready to let go.
Not long from now, you'll leave me;
This too, I've come know.

From you and me against the world, to your standing on your own-
So much has changed while you've grown.
Have compassion for my heart;
Please don't rush to leave me alone.

Understand this, my child, my pride and joy…
I saw this day coming when you were a small boy.
Living in each moment this far-
I come here unprepared.
Knowing it would come,
Unexpected sadness, a consideration I'd not dared.

The time draws near to my letting go-
I know…
Please, my son, don't hurry it along.
Give me some time, one last year…
This letting go, is not easy for me, because you're so dear.

Each day is a new beginning…

~~~

In that far off sweet forever,
Just beyond the shining river…
Thinking of the love that's gone away -
Dreaming of yesterday.

As the years going flying by,
I think of yesterday and want to cry.

Every day is filled with disappointment -
Feelings of great resentment.

Why can't things be like before?
When will he walk through my door…
Whispering words, I've heard before,
"I love you, and will, forever more."

~~~
## *All Aboard*

Each morning I wake to board my private car.
I know not how high it will take me, or how far.
Some days it holds me at its peak,
Leaving me weak,
For an uncomfortable stay..
Plummeting to earth for me to find my way.

I am not the conductor of this roller coaster -
Velocity and pitch are at his command.
Each day I ride with a white knuckled hand.

Its speed and force sometimes crest my fears.
Leaving me alone to dry my tears.
At times, it takes me higher than my heart can imagine real.
Allying my fright, permitting me to heal.

I often wish for a more steady course.
But he is the pilot, and the direction source.

~~~

Born to be abused.
Not my body…
My soul is bruised.
My confidence ebbs,
My esteem is dead,
Every bit of it old news.

Nothing I do is good enough or right.
Just another thing about which to fight.
I keep paying my dues.

Is death the answer, to end the pain?
There is much to lose, is there anything to gain?

It wouldn't hurt so much, if I were the only target.
My child suffers too -
Can he ever forget?

I did leave once, though that effort was in vain.
He tricked me to return, just to hurt me again.

The Road

It is a twisted path, on a never-ending road…
Where does it lead?
Will I ever know?
Following it,
Forever wandering
Forever wondering…
Where will it take me?

These thoughts baffle my brain.
Experiencing new thoughts, ideas, what next?
What else will I find?
What else is to be seen?
What is the answer?
What does it all mean?

Days and weeks go by.
As my life ticks away, I think with a sigh…
Will I come to the end, or no…?
When will I find the end to this road?

~~~

You are the child I thought I'd never see.
For years I'd dreamed of you,
Though your father eluded me.

News of you brought forth in me such a joyous feeling.
The thought of you, my dream come true -
Leaving my head reeling.

I loved you so much, even before first-sight.
My holiday baby, born Thanksgiving night.

God blessed me with you after many long years.
I give thanks to Him each day… for listening when I pray-
For all the laughter and tears…

You are my little Dudie,
That you'll always be…
I praise the Lord for sending you to me.

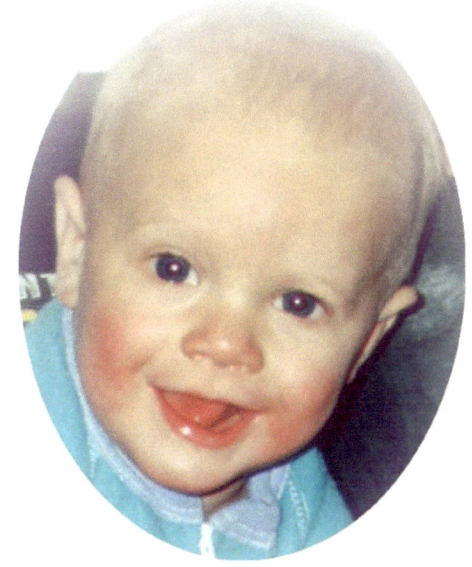

~~~~
### *Thirty*

Deep and dark are my thoughts -
Sometimes a mystery, even to me.
All I know is that I'm stuck in a place
I don't want to be.

Each day brings a new battle I must fight.
Dreams, they torment me, with the birth of the night.

I need a change, new faces, a new scene…
A place to clear my head,
To discern what it all means.

I need to relax, to free my soul…
But how do I escape this vacuous hole?

### *Morning*

The rays of Sol, shine bright and strong.
Birds sounding a glorious song.
The cool glimmer of grass wet with dew -
''Tis the day… beautiful and new.

The sun warms my sleepy face.
Not yet ready to join the human race…
I'll sit and enjoy my coffee.
I feel alive and free.

How soothing, the crickets, the birds -
Their melodies, the best, those without words.
The music created relaxes the mind.
Any more beautiful you'll not find.

This pace, the one I find ideal…
For this to me is what I call real.

## *No More*

You'll make me cry no more!
Never again shall I fall in love.
You see my friend this is why,
You'll never again make me cry…

To love and not be loved is the pain of pains.
Like being bound by unbreakable chains.
Wanting closeness -
Getting only distance.

To be free of love's crushing hold…
Once again to be brave and bold…
Never love again; mend my broken heart.
Find a new path; make a fresh start.

Wanting no more sorrow…
New love comes; shall I pass it by?
Will life then be, nothing more than a lie?

Is love essential to live day by day?
Or can we live without it and be happy anyway?
I may never forget my love for you as the years pass by…
But never again, will you make me cry.

~~~~

I am thinking about you today.
There are so many things I know not how to say.
Nor where to begin - should I keep silent?
My mind is stretched so thin; my emotions violent...
Inside me.
Through the years, my love for you has only grown.
A love like this, I have never before known.
Yet I am uncertain - Doubt, a heavy curtain...
around my heart.
I pray, Dear God, why?
If my love for him will never die -
Our love truly is meant to be...
Why does he not feel the same for me?
By your side I will always stand.
Forever taking you by the hand-
In love and comfort till the end of time.
I need no reason or rhyme...
I love you.
Want for your happiness is all I see.
But does it lie with me?
If you love me, let me know.
Speak the words; let it show... that my heart can heal.
I have forgiveness and given it freely.
Forgetting though, is not so easy.
Apprehension slips in, leaving me racked with pain.
Questions mark my mind like a bloody stain...
Will he leave me again?
If you love me, let me know.
Speak the words; let it show.
I need reassurance that can come only from you.
Help me to know that your heart is true.

In Perfect Harmony

Winter is coming to an end.
Soon its might shall weaken and bend.
Still fighting for its right to be…
Blowing snow can we yet see.
The snow will melt -
The sun's warmth will be felt.
Yes, spring is on its way.
Like a rainbow will come the flowers of May.
Life now, born anew.
Under beautiful skies of blue;
Baby beings of every breed,
Flowers and ferns from every seed,
The air fragrant, crisp, and clean -
Not an angry cloud to be seen…
Birds abreast the lofty breeze -
Help us forget the winter freeze.
And to be heard, doth the voice of spring,
Express itself in the songs they sing.
As I behold the wonderful things, I see…
I realize life, in perfect harmony.

Playing the Game

Oh the gray days, they seem to go on endlessly.
Every action a reaction, to the routine.
All the faces so different,
Yet all the same.
Wanting, and whining and playing the game.

Can I help you?
What would you like?
A bit of elixir to make you feel all right?

I'll assist you in your escape,
But there is none for me.
Oh the gray days… they go on endlessly.

~~~

I really don't know how I feel.
All of this seems incredibly surreal.
Has my worst nightmare come true?

I don't know what to think, say, or how to act.
Do I advance, or should I retract?

I am sick inside; I cannot eat.
Completely exhausted, I cannot sleep.

My hands are shaking, as I write this here.
The fog so dense, nothing's clear.

I have so much love in my heart to give…
Without him, I don't ever want to live.

Beauty All Around Me

There is beauty all around me.
From the earth beneath my feet, to the sky above my head,
As far as the eye can see.

Majestic mountains kiss the heavens with snow-covered peaks.
Eagles take wing...
Animals play hide-and-seek.

The sunshine is warm on my face today...
A few clouds dot the sky.
Why… it is a beautiful day.

No matter how off-balance my life can be some of the time -
Not a moment passes that I am not thankful, for that which I can call mine.

I appreciate all of my life experiences -
Good or ill, they've moved me to progress.
Without each and every one of them, I'd simply not be myself; and that is my success.

Life only happens to you if you give it permission.
I choose to make life happen for me...
Not cower in submission.

Strong and tall do I stand, yet yielding can I be.
I love my life so tremendously... I see beauty all around me.

Wherever I go... whomever I meet -
Nowhere else on earth, could ever be so sweet.

I love you my family, my home and my friends.

I Said Good-bye Today

The only constant in the universe is change.
For good or bad, it matters not.
Today it just seems strange -
I feel I've lost a lot.

I said good-bye to my child this morn.
He spread his wings and flew from here.
I knew it would come, since the day he was born.
I knew I could not keep him forever so near.

The tears want to come, but I try not to let them.
Tears of pride or sorrow I do not know…
Boys have a way of becoming men -
So now, I must let go.

God bless and keep you, my beloved son.

I'll always be with you and you in my heart.

You are meant for great things; they must be done.

Never forget where you got your start.

~~~

If there must be ugliness in order to have beauty and if beauty is truly in the eye of the beholder; then isn't ugliness beautiful?

~~~

Beauty is the sun glistening off dew damp leaves,
A weeping willow dancing in the breeze -
Sounds of forest creatures in harmony.

The sun setting upon crystal waters -
The tranquility of a walk along a quiet seashore…
The sparkle in a child's eye -
It is a smile.
Two young lovers holding hands.
Beauty is peace and it is everywhere.

My Life
Brainwashed by abuse

A constant struggle to hide,
From what I thought was my darker side.
No confidence that I ever was right,
So I'd run away from the fight.
Afraid of myself and the world out there…
I built me a fortress and would not share.
One day he came knocking; I opened the door.
He touched me in ways I'd not known before.
I felt good for a while, but in stepped self-doubt.
Before I knew it, I'd shut him out.
I would try many times to re-open that door.
But in blew that doubt to slam it once more.
Now his arms they grow tired,
His knuckles, they do bleed,
As his love for me slowly goes to seed.
I have found the courage to open that door, to fling it wide.
Now he knows not if he wants what's inside.
He tried so hard and waited so long,
For me to see how I was wrong.
I now know that all I thought my dark side,
Was just my humanity and nothing to hide.
I ran from the goodness in me, for I thought I had none.
Now I know better, still my life is undone.
I accept the imperfection that I am, and myself I forgive.
Now I am ready to begin to live.

~~~~
## Ten Years

Ten years of my life have passed by.
I reflect on them all, break down, and cry.
I weep for the failure,
I weep for the fights,
I weep for the good times,
I weep for the nights.
Was it time wasted?
I think no.
For it I've got beautiful memories and a child to show.
My life is so different; it will never be the same.
Now I'm a new player, and I don't know the game.
Songs that I hear, places that I go…
Bring back memories of the love we used to know.
Ten years of my life have passed by the way -
If only I could turn back time to a better day.

## Wonder Why

Here I sit and wonder why,
Love has bloomed, withered, and died.
Ire's flared and harsh words spoken -
Love is lost and hearts are broken.
Sadness abounds - the air is thick.
Enough anger and pain to make one sick.
Alone I'll stand, for it's best, I see…
That now, at the edge, solitude is what I need.
Today starts a journey into a brand new life.
It's best for all; I'm no longer his wife.
A role I played ten years and failed.
Like sunken ships that should not have sailed.
My ray of sunshine, my only joy;
The brilliance and laughter that is my little boy.
Yet alone I sit, and wonder why,
The pain remains as the days pass by.

~~~

Out of the blue and into the black,
The darkness hides from me, where I am at.
What once seemed clear now escapes my grasp.
Slipping swiftly through my fingers -
Sand through an hourglass.

My tearful eyes no longer see light.
When comes the end of this dreadful night?

I fear misstepping in this shadow land.
If only, there were someone to take my hand.
Is there a path to walk, in this place of pain?
Shall I be forever sentenced to remain?

One day at a time is now a luxury for me.
Moment by moment I live, for my sanity.

## *People*

Life is full of people, stabbing you in the back.
To whom are you to turn?
Will you take another burn?
Are you anyone's concern?
Will you suffer another attack?

They can treat you so bad and walk all over you.
Isn't it sad?
Is anyone true?
Are there any good people around?
Why all this bullshit…?
Where's a friend to be found?

## *Wee Lass*

See the wee lass, sitting by the shore.
See the wee lass, who knows not where she's headed anymore.

See the wee lass, sitting by the bay.
See the wee lass, who knows no happiness this day.

See the wee lass weeping on her bed.
See the wee lass, the voices screaming inside her head.

See the wee lass, waiting for her sunshine to return at the end of the day.
See the wee lass, longing to hear her lover say,
"Everything will be okay."

## *Words of Gold*

Last night I saw it in a dream…
Truths and lies only half yet told -
Beautiful memories and words of gold.
In your absence, happiness is lacking in my days.
I mask the emptiness with people, parties, and haze.
Finding temporary pleasure,
Not my true heart's desire.

A soul that sings when love is close by -
One that could rejoice if it were here you'd stay.
Eyes that see only through tears, when you're away.

To you, I gave my heart and soul -
Yet too late am I to fulfill your needs.
For this failure, my poor heart bleeds.

It is you with whom I wish to walk eternity's roads.
Take me into your home, your life…
Let me forever be, your faithful loving wife.
I want you; I need you, and can't live without you.
Oh how I long to say, "I do."

## *Let Me Be*

During the day, I sit in school.
All the jocks are in class,
While my friends have fun.
Nope, no heads in class;
I'm the only one.

Life is no fun, when there are rules to go by.
Why can't I be left alone, to learn by myself?
Just let me fly.

I want to be free to learn from my mistakes, to do as I wish…
Without punishment, or ridicule…
I know I'm not perfect, but I'm also no fool.

Let me be who I want to be!
I want to be me; I want to be free!

~~~~
Burn Out

I feel so dazed and confused.
Feeling mistreated and mentally abused.
I feel so lonely, like my friends have cast me aside.
I just want to run away -
Curl up and hide.
I need someone who cares, someone to help.

Get me through these darkened days -
My good ol' dope.
Will I die not knowing any other hope?
Please help me out of this distorted, mixed up life -
Out of this insanity…
All I see is the knife.
The world is closing in on me,
I want to get out!
Please stop this shit, before I burn out!

~~~~
Drugs

Cocaine snorted up the nose, short circuits the brain.
Heroin is shot up the vein.
Smoke dope, until your eyes are totally red -
Eat acid 'til you're messed up in the head.
Drink and drink 'til you're totally wasted.
Bacardi and Pepsi are good to be tasted.
Watch Out! Hold On! Take it easy on the drugs.
Soon your head will hold cosmic space bugs.

Days Rage

Wake in the morning, and fall out of bed.
Get to your feet and throw back your head.
Walk to the bathroom; now face the face.
Looking pretty bad - the night you can't erase.
It never lies…
That looking glass.
Proof positive -
You were wasted off your ass.

This is your day.
This is your rage.
Your life is a story.
Time to turn the page.

You walk out the door; the sun hits your eyes.
You smell the filth; hear the noise…
Once again, a part of you dies.

Your eyes start to water; your nose begins to run.
It's time to get out.
What happened to all the fun?

Go back inside, do a line, or have a drink.
The knock on the door makes you shake and shrink.
Forget the knock and flick on the tube.
Shut out the world and smoke another doob.

This is your day.
This is your rage.
Your life is your story…
Time to turn the page.
Each day you go through your own little Hell…
Buddy, keep payin' your dues.
It's the same ol' shit… Nothing but bad news.

Understanding Domestic Abuse: Why Does She Stay?

One of the most devastating misconceptions that many people have about domestic abuse is the notion that the abuse must not be real, or serious, if she doesn't leave. I'd say that it is safe to say that the question that many need an answer to is... Why does she stay.

It is fairly common, for outsiders to look down their noses in judgmental fashion, at a woman, simply because she stays in the abusive environment. I wonder how many of these same people feel abused at their place of employment, yet continue to work there.

Women do not stay in abusive relationships because they enjoy, or accept the abuse.

Women stay in abusive relationships because of: Fear, Guilt, Financial dependence, Religious beliefs, Denial, to name just a few.

What does she fear? A woman fears many things, while inside an abusive relationship. Many women fear that their desire to leave will be discovered and any attempt at leaving will fail. Abused women have usually become isolated from family members, friends, and other people who may be able to offer support, so she fears not having help, before, during, or after leaving.

These women fear being found, brought back, and punished for having tried to leave their abuser. They fear for their safety as well as that of their children. To defy an abusive partner is dangerous business.

For some, they have not been permitted to work outside the home, nor have access to family finances; they feel financially trapped. Where is she to go without money or access to it?

The psychological abuse that women endure is a major factor in why she stays. She has been programmed, by her abuser, that all the problems within the relationship are her fault. This is where guilt enters the stage.

She may feel guilty for not being able to make her husband happy enough, her own abuse, for not being able to protect her children, and guilty for every negative thing she has ever heard her abuser say. When you hear negative things about yourself, long enough, whether they are true or not, you come to believe them as truth.

Along with that, religious beliefs can inspire a tremendous amount of guilt. I'm not a good wife... I'm not a good mother... I should be submissive to my husband, etc... Let's face it... there are religions that actually condone beating a wife for disobedience.

Finally, some battered women don't realize they're being abused, simply because they have not sustained physical injury. Not every battered woman is beaten.

I am not a battered woman... He's never actually hit me... He just says things he doesn't mean when he's angry, drunk or high...

Domestic abuse and violence are not synonymous. All women who have been beaten have been emotionally/psychologically abused (*battered*), but not all emotionally/psychologically abused women have been beaten. Sadly, those who have been physically assaulted are one up on those who wear their scars on the inside. Physical abuse produces physical evidence. Emotional abuse does not. Therefore, *physical abuse* can be reported and punished; not so for *emotional/psychological abuse*.

So, why do women stay? Because they feel damned if they do, and damned if they don't. Without support and resources they are stuck.

No one deserves to be abused... NOT EVER.

Copyright © 2007 The Trii-Zine Ezine www.ezines1.com Trina L.C. Sonnenberg

About the Author

Trina L.C. Sonnenberg, owner of TLC Promotions, is a freelance writer, and the publisher of The Trii-Zine Ezine; an Internet marketing electronic magazine, as well as AdsOnQ, an article marketing RSS feed. She lives in the sleepy little town of Nucla, Colorado, with her husband, Jeff, son, Tanner, and her mother, Mary. Nucla is located in the foothills of the San Juan Mountains: in the southwestern part of the state.

A domestic abuse survivor, Trina used writing as a coping mechanism during her years of abuse. This book is the result of that personal struggle and has been published as a way of offering solidarity and hope to others who are in a similar situation.

All of the photographs, contained in this book, were taken in southwestern Colorado, in and around the San Juan Mountains.

Copyright © 2007

www.ingramcontent.com/pod-product-compliance
Lightning Source LLC
Chambersburg PA
CBHW042026150426
43198CB00002B/84